A LITTLE HISTORY OF IRELAND

SEAMUS MAC CALL

A LITTLE HISTORY OF
IRELAND

with a final chapter by
CATHERINE MAC CALL
and
BÖRJE THILMAN

A DOLMEN PRESS BOOK
North America: Irish Books and Media

A Little History of Ireland is set in Baskerville type and set and printed in the Republic of Ireland at Leinster Leader Ltd., Naas, for the publishers,
The Dolmen Press Limited, Mountrath, Portlaoise, Ireland

North America: Irish Books and Media,
683 Osceola Avenue, Saint Paul Minnesota 55105, USA.

Edited by Catherine MacCall
Designed by Liam Miller

First published 1973
Reset and reprinted 1976
Reprinted 1980
US edition 1980
New edition 1982: additional text by Catherine MacCall and Borje Thilman.

BRITISH LIBRARY CATALOGUING IN PUBLICATION DATA
MacCall, Seamus
    A little history of Ireland.
    I. Ireland — History
    1. Title
    941.5   DA910

ISBN 0 85105 400 5 The Dolmen Press
ISBN 0 937702 01 3 Irish Books and Media

Library of Congress Catalogue Card No. 82-82419

CONTENTS

When History Began	7
History in Legend	9
Irish Expansion	10
Contributions to Civilization	12
Sea-cast Floods of Foreigners	14
Clontarf	15
The Normans	16
The Statute of Kilkenny	17
Poynings' Laws	18
Henry VIII	19
The Plantation Policy	20
Scorched Earth	22
The Third Plantation of Ulster	23
Ireland Rises Again	25
The Parliamentarians	26
Cromwell	27
James and William	28
The Penal Laws	31
Ireland Overseas	32
Legislative Independence	33
Ireland and France	35
The Famine	37
The Fenians	39

The Unionists   40

Home Rule   41

The Irish Volunteers   42

The Easter Rising   43

The First Dáil   44

The Government of Ireland Act   46

Disgracing the Name of Britain   47

Uneasy Peace   48

The Free State and The Republic   51

The Republic of Ireland   55

Index   57

A LITTLE HISTORY
OF IRELAND

WHEN HISTORY BEGAN in Ireland three main racial strains were already playing their various parts in the shaping of what today is the oldest nation in Western Europe.

The first of the three had begun with an off-shoot of the long-headed, long-limbed, Cro-Magnon race which came to Europe from North Africa in the Stone Age.

Next in point of time had come the 'Mediterraneans', another long-headed, though shorter-statured race, known on the Continent to Roman chroniclers as the *Iberni,* and in Ireland to Irish chroniclers as the *Uib-Ernai,* or 'descendants of Eire', an ancient fertility goddess whose name means 'noble'. To them Ireland owes its ancient name Eire, the oldest existing national name in the world, but corrupted in comparatively recent times by the addition of the word 'land' and the subsequent dropping of the initial 'E'. Though concentrated largely in the West and South during the Bronze Age the *Uib-Ernai,* or Eireans, represented the bulk of the population of both Ireland and Scotland in early historical times.

In the fourth century B.C., came still another long-headed race, the Celts, or Gauls, who brought with them the Iron-Age culture of the Continent and certain characteristic excellencies in the arts of peace and of war. The most notable of the tangible features of early Celtic culture —the basic elements of their artistic conceptions— can be traced back to the region of the Caspian Sea. From there strong migratory currents carried these influences as far as the Valley of the Danube, following in the wake of the herdsmen and shepherds who, somewhere about 2,000 B.C., had carried to that area the early off-shoot of the Aryan language which we know as Celtic. The Valley of the Danube thus became the cradle of what, even at that early stage, might be called the Celtic nation. From philological evidence, we know that somewhere about 1,000 B.C. the Celts overflowed northwards into the territory of the Germanic tribes and, from the evidence of Celtic words which have passed into German, it is possible to see that the Germanic peoples derived considerable advantage from the association; the German words for nation, King and magistrate, certain German terms relating to law and government, to social organization, to land and houses, to agriculture, medicine and metal working, and the names of many articles of food and clothing, being derived from the Celtic. In the sixth century B.C., inundations of the sea in the Baltic area and subsequent revolt of the still-racially distinct Germanic tribes caused the Northern Celts to withdraw across the Rhine. Then, spreading over territory now represented by Belgium and Northern France, they came into contact with other Celtic peoples established along the valleys of the Seine and the Marne. It is to this period of conflicting expansion that we date the beginning of the migration which provided Ireland with its Celtic colonists of the fourth century B.C. By this time, there had ceased to be such a thing as a pure race; the Celts were already something of a mixture and at least two of the racial elements in their composition were not vastly different to what were already established in Ireland. But, as a part of an already well-defined Celtic civilization, they brought with them those elements of artistic achievement which, after many vicissitudes, were to reach their highest development in the ornamentation of the *Book of Kells* and in the sculptured crosses which are a characteristic feature of early Christian civilization in Ireland and which, on the other side of the

Irish Sea, still stand to mark the progress of Irish missionary endeavour in Britain.

The Irish bards and *seanachies,* to whom we owe the picturesque 'invasion legends' which are a colourful part of early Irish literature, acknowledged the tradition of the three main racial elements in the Irish Nation by naming them respectively the *Fir Bolg,* or 'men of the quiver' (i.e. 'bow-men'), the *Fir Domhnann,* or 'men of the territory' in contra-distinction to 'foreigners', and the *Fir Gaileoin* — a name obviously inspired by their Gaulish origin. In a still later age the *seanachies* re-named these same three racial elements, again respectively, the 'Sons of Ir', the 'Sons of Eber' and the 'Sons of Ermon'. This time, however, an already existing semblance of national unity led them to attribute a common origin to all three in an ancestor to whom they gave the name *Mileadh* or Milesius. And to be on the safe side in the matter of nomenclature, they also provided as ancestors a certain Gadelius and a lady named Scota, thus explaining to their own satisfaction the then synonymous national names of Gael and Scot.

The oldest of the more genuinely historical Irish sagas tells the story of the coming of the iron-age Celts. It explains that it was from the iron-bladed spears, or *laighens,* with which the Gauls were armed that the province of Leinster derived its name. It tells us, also, that the invasion was a purely masculine one and since the invaders were thus obliged to seek their wives among the earlier 'Eirean' inhabitants — a fact borne out by archaeological evidence — there was a consequent fusion of culture and a consequent interchange of manners and customs.

Irish sagas relating to events of the first century B.C. —

9

the heroic deeds of the 'Knights of the Red Branch' of the North and of the similar chivalric brotherhoods of the West and the South — provide us with some of the finest epic material in the whole world of literature. And the great tales of Conaire Mór, king of Ireland in the second century A.D., and the better-known stories of Goll MacMorna and Fionn MacCumhail (Finn Mac Cool), picture for us an Ireland with a population already moulded into something approaching a mental unity and with a culture already distinctively national.

According to Ptolemy, the second-century Greek geographer, Ireland in his time already possessed ten 'cities', two of them termed 'illustrious', and of these one corresponds with the location of Tara, the historic capital of early Ireland and the setting of many of the finest pieces of early Irish literature.

Patrick Pearse, writing in 1912, said that had Irish literature been rediscovered four centuries ago, instead of Greek and Latin literature, modern letters might have received a nobler, because more humane, inspiration than they did actually receive. He believed that Irish literature was more heroic and at the same time more gentle than the old Greek literature, that its inspiration of chivalry and spirituality made it more delicate and mystical. And certainly we know, from internal evidence in plenty, that it influenced the Irish mind with a whole lot of colour and fantasy, of chivalry and humanity, of pitiful tragedy and exultant romance.

IRISH EXPANSION

But the heroic content of early Irish literature was a national inspiration of a more assertive kind. Throughout the Bronze Age, as throughout the Stone Age, there was considerable migration from Ireland to Scotland and thence as far as Scandinavia. It is also known that

Scotland continued to be colonized from Ireland throughout the distinctively Irish phases of the Iron Age and, in the literature of events as far back as the first century B.C., Scotland and Ireland are shown as sharing a common language, common social customs and a common cultural development.

Then came the Roman conquest of Southern Britian; and Roman chroniclers were soon complaining that warriors from Ireland and Scotland — under the collective name of Scottas, Scoti or Scots — were making something of a habit of raiding the Roman settlements.

The Irish chronicles of these events begin with Crimthann the Third, king of Ireland about the middle of the fourth century, for it was he who led the first really well-authenticated attacks on Roman Britian, his known settlements ranging from Dunadd in Argyle to Glastonbury in Somerset. The Irish Sea was already truly Irish. 'The Scot moved all Ireland', says the Roman poet Claudian, 'and the sea foamed under the weight of his hostile oars'.

Crimthann died in 375 but his place was soon taken by Niall. St. Patrick tells us, in his own 'Confession', that when he himself was carried off to Ireland — probably from somewhere near the Bristol Channel — he was one of 'so many thousands' of captives. Furthermore, the Romans themselves record the destruction, during Niall's reign, of all the principal Roman stations between the Severn and the Dee. And in the since-discovered hoards of Roman coins, hidden away by citizens who died not return or survive to recover them, the evidence can be read of the destruction of such Brito-Roman towns as Chester, Wroxeter, Caerleon-on-Usk and Caerwent. On the further evidence of the latest coins in the hoards it is possible to fix the date of their destruction as immediately subsequent to 395.

In the following year Stilicho gathered together a new

army for a new war against the Irish invaders. And the Roman poet Claudian flattered his patrons by singing tirumphantantly about Ireland 'mourning her mounds of dead'. But the Venerable Bede, with less poetic licence, says: 'The insolent Irish invaders returned home only to come again after no long interval.' A few years later the Romans abandoned Britain altogether.

During the next century in Britain there were, in addition to the arrival of new invaders — Angles, Jutes, Frisians and Saxons — continued raids and further colonizations by the old invaders. And in 498 there was a new and large-scale Irish colonization of Scotland. This was led by a grandson of King Niall, Fergus Mór MacEarca, who became the first absolute king of Scotland and thereby established the royal line of Scotland.

CONTRIBUTIONS TO CIVILIZATION

At home, having been spared conquest by the Romans, the Irish had passed through a phase of clan socialism and had become a heptarchy, with semi-independent rulers in seven co-ordinate kingdoms, all (according to tradition) acknowledging the *Ard Rí,* or High King of Tara, as head of the confederacy. By this time, Ireland had also evolved a legal system with laws regulating almost everything from the conduct of doctors, judges, teachers, public hospitalers and builders, to the duties of foster-parents and foster-children.

The middle of the fifth century saw the introduction of Christianity into Ireland and the following century was notable for more peaceful invasions of Britain. Of these the first was led by Colm Cille — later to be known as St. Columba. He established the first Christian monastery on Iona and, some fifty years before St. Augustine came to England from Rome, began the task which was to make that little Scottish Island a fount of learning and the sacred resting place of more kings than have ever been gathered together, before or since, alive or dead, anywhere else in the world. Other Irish monks carried the teachings of Christianity as far as Iceland — possibly as far as American according to some Mexican traditions — and eastwards across the North Sea to almost every ravaged land in Europe. The German scholar, Zimmer, speaks of the old Irish monks as 'instructors in every known branch of the science and learning of their time'. They were, he says, 'the possessors and bearers of a higher culture than was to be found anywhere on the Continent', and to them he accords the honour of having laid 'the corner-stone of western culture on the Continent'.

In the year 635, Aidan and a few other Irish monks set out from Iona to convert the English — 'a barbarous, stiff-necked, intractable race' — and at the request of the king of Northumbria established a first monastery at Lindisfarne. They carried with them the art of illumination and the Irish script, a cursive adaptation of the Latin alphabet. It was through the medium of the Irish script that reading and writing were brought into use among the English; the earliest extant MS of the earliest English epic, 'Beowulf', and the early Anglo-Saxon chronicles being written in what today, in a slightly modified form, is still the Irish alphabet.

Cuthbert, Colman, Cedd, Dicoil, Diuma (who founded the first monastery at Peterborough, 'The cradle of Christianity' in central England), and Maoldubh, (who founded the great monastic school of Malmesbury), are a few among the other Irish monks who 'were led by God's providence to England'.

On the Continent, the fifth-century Irish monk, Siadhal (Sedulius), wrote the great Christian epic 'Carmen Paschale'. Columban (St. Columbanus) established the French monastery at Luxeuil, converted

German tribes along the Rhine, and, crossing the Alps, established at Bobbio 'a focus of knowledge and instruction'. Fearghal (St. Virgilius), who converted the Bavarians, was the first scholar to teach that the earth was round.

Fursa established monasteries at Peronne and St. Quentin. Fridolin became the first bishop of Strasbourg. Clemens and Albinus, 'two Scots from Ireland', became advisers to Charlemagne. Damhnaith (St. Dympna), an Irish nun, has her shrine at Gheel in Belgium. Lévin (St. Livinus) was martyred in the Netherlands. Donatus was made bishop of Fiesole, in 824, simply because he 'came from Ireland'. Fiachra (St. Fiacre) had his shrine near Paris and is still prayed to by French gardeners in need of rain and Killian became patron saint of Wurzburg.

So the list might go on. And it was not in religious zeal alone that the untold multitude of great Irish scholars found an outlet for their greatness. The French authority, Montalembert, has paid tribute to their work in a more material sphere: 'It is due to their untiring energy that half of France and of ungrateful Europe has been restored to cultivation.'

SEA-CAST FLOODS OF FOREIGNERS

But in the eighth century the tide of invasion turned and 'there came great sea-cast floods of foreigners into Eire, so that there was no port thereof without a fleet'. These foreigners, the Norsemen, burned out the great schools of Armagh and the monastic settlements of Kildare and Glendalough in 774. They destroyed Clonmacnoise on the Shannon in 777. There was a second destruction of St. Brigid's original establishment in Kildare in 778 and of Armagh in 783. In 787 there was wholesale massacre and destruction in St. Columba's old establishment in Derry. The following year there was a burning of

14

churches and monasteries at Clonard and Clonfert. The gospel books, the illuminated manuscripts which had long been a part of the equipment of the Irish missioners and had acquired a tradition of miraculous holiness which remained long after the monks themselves had perished, were now destroyed in hundreds, partly as a planned campaign on behalf of the Scandinavian gods and partly to make 'cures' for a variety of diseases.

CLONTARF

Some respite came as the result of a spectacular Irish victory over the invaders, and of the subsequent need of the Sacndinavians to withdraw forces from Ireland to strengthen their hold on England. The period which followed, known to Irish historians as 'the forty years' rest', was notable for a revival of religious and intellectual activity. But there were still Scandinavian settlements at various places on the Irish coast and new invasions soon ushered in a new era of cruelty and gloom in which Norsemen, Danes and Irish were spasmodically engaged until well into the second half of the tenth century. Then, out of the turmoil, there arose several great Irish leaders. One of these was Murtagh who equipped a thousand Irish warriors with leather cloaks and in the depth of winter fought Norse and Danes wherever they declined to acknowledge his authority. Chief among the others were Maelseachlain (Malachi), Mahon and Brian Boru who all contended vigorously against the invaders, pushing them back to their several strongholds on the coast and paving the way for Brian's decisive victory at Clontarf, near Dublin, in 1014.

For this last great battle, Sacndinavians from Britain and from faraway Iceland had rallied to the support of their countrymen in Ireland and their defeat practically put an end to the Viking raids. Danish kings ruled in Britain and Danes were settled in Northern France. But in Ireland, though many of the Scandinavians remained as settlers and were eventually absorbed into the Irish nation, they ceased to be a political force.

THE NORMANS

In 1066 the Danes of France, now known as Normans, conquered England. And in 1170 Norman knights with an army of Flemings came to Ireland where, aided by a deposed king of Leinster, they captured Waterford, Wexford and Dublin and took nominal possession of Leinster.

For another century the Normans fought to establish themselves throughout Ireland but, though greatly aided by Papal edicts of excommunication against all Irish chiefs who refused to submit to the Anglo-Norman king Henry II, they were never wholly successful.

On the Irish side, due largely to local rivalries and the disruptive effects of the earlier prolonged struggle for survival, the war against the Normans was little more than a war of clans. But, eventually, some of the Irish leaders saw the need for troops regularly trained for war and always available for service. This led to the establishment of standing armies, recruited in Ireland and in the Gaelic areas of Scotland, the former being generally the *ciartharnagh* (anglicized 'kernes') and the latter the more heavily-armed *gall-oglaigh* (anglicized 'gallow-glasses').

In the meantime, many of the Normans who had succeeded in establishing themselves among the Irish had taken Irish wives and had become 'more Irish than the Irish themselves'.

The re-absorption of Normandy into the kingdom of France further accentuated this break with old loyalties and later English efforts to conquer Ireland were opposed by many of the Irish-Normans, as well as by the Irish themselves. Nevertheless, quarrels among the local Norman lords and occasional quick changes of allegiance eventually served to strengthen England's hold on Ireland and permitted an enlargement of England's sphere of influence.

THE STATUTE OF KILKENNY

In 1367 the English were able to summon a 'parliament' at Kilkenny and there they passed laws forbidding their colonists, under penalty of forfeiting their land, to speak Irish, to Gaelicize their names, to wear Irish costume, play Irish games, entertain Irish bards and poets or ride horseback in the Irish fashion. To marry with the Irish, or to have recourse to Irish law, were declared 'treasonable' offences. This anti-Irish malignity even extended to the Church; no benefice was to be conferred upon any but English-speakers; no Irish were to be received into any cathedral chapter; and, within the English settlements, no Irishman was to be allowed to enter any abbey, monastery or religious order.

In its intentions the Statute of Kilkenny admitted the impossibility of conquering the Irish people and sought for a while to consolidate the position of English subjects in Ireland as a foreign element, confined to such garrisoned towns as Wexford, Kilkenny, Waterford, New Ross and Carlow and to an 'English Pale', which area, under the control of England, though it still stretched from just south of Dublin to Dundalk, had been recently reduced by Irish victories at Downpatrick and Carrickfergus and by a retreat of the English through the Mourne Mountains and a further defeat near Dundalk.

A few years after the passing of the Statute of Kilkenny, Art MacMurrogh Cavanagh, a recently elected king of Leinster, showed his contempt for its provisions by marrying the daughter of an Anglo-Norman lord. The English government in Dublin thereupon seized the lands to which the lady was heiress and Art MacMurrogh Cavanagh replied by waging relentless war against the occupation forces until only a small territory around Dublin and a few isolated towns on the coast remained in English hands.

In 1417 Art MacMurrogh Cavanagh was disposed of by poisoning. No immediate follower arose to lead the final effort which would have extinguished the power of England in Ireland and, as a result of the impotence of the puppet parliament which England had established in Dublin, there followed a period of decentralization in which chiefs of territories lived independently, among their own people, sharing a unified culture but fighting occasionally with their neighbours and making little or no contribution towards a unified national policy. And when, out of this chaotic state of affairs, one Irish-Norman lord, Earl Thomas of Desmond, rose to sufficient power to alarm the English, the latter resorted to the expedient of 'adopting' him, as 'Lord Deputy', to rule a semi-independent Ireland in the name of the English king.

POYNINGS' LAWS

The fall of the Yorkist dynasty, as a result of the 'War of the Roses', brought about changed conditions in Ireland as in England. The new Lancastrian dynasty largely represented the merchant classes in England while such royalist sympathy as there was in Ireland was on the side of the defeated Yorkists and the old nobility. To assert his authority the Lancastrian king Henry VII sent over a new Lord Deputy, Sir Edward Poynings, who summoned a new parliament and passed new anti-Irish laws.

Already in the course of the fifteenth century there had

18

been a variety of admissions of England's inability either to destroy or to conquer the Irish people. But, to hide this failure, there had been a variety of enactments designed to 'disguise' the Irish as English. So far as English law could run, the Irish had been forbidden to wear Irish dress, grow moustaches or use their Irish names — and, instead of their Irish names, they had been ordered to use 'translations' or alternatively 'to take unto themselves the name of the English town, or of a trade, or a colour'. In 1465 rewards were legalized for the killing of any Irishman who, by failure to obey these decrees, proclaimed himself as proudly Irish. Ponyning' Parliament, though it abandoned as hopeless the effort to eradicate the Gaelic language, confirmed most of the other enactments and further decreed that all laws recently passed in England should apply also to Ireland and that no laws should be passed by the 'colonial' parliament in Ireland without the prior sanction of the English king and his Privy Council.

HENRY VIII

Following his break with Rome, Henry VIII assumed the title of 'King of Ireland' and, in English law, Ireland thus became a subordinate kingdom. War against the English in Ireland thereby became 'rebellion' and neither the 'Poynings' English' nor the 'mere Irish' and neither the Irish-Norman nor the 'old English' were to enjoy rights other than those accorded them by English law.

Efforts to impose the new order had already provoked the rebellion of 'Silken' Thomas Fitzgerald. Its failure had been followed by an English punitive expedition into the Irish midlands and the south. Much destruction of property and more miseries for the Irish people were the only results of the expedition. The English viceroy, Lord Leonard Green, paid for his failure with his head.

19

By this time the Reformation had reached Ireland. At first it made little headway but a number of Irish chiefs — notably the O'Donnell, the O'Neill, the Mac Carthy Mór, the MacCarthy Reagh, the MacMahon, the O'Brien, the O'Moore, the O'Rourke and the O'Sullivan Beara — now repudiated the authority of the Pope. And an influential number of Irish chiefs agreed to hold their land 'as from the King'. But these personal 'submissions' were, to the Irish, merely agreements between individuals. Irish chiefs — and even Irish kings — held 'elective appointments' and under Irish law they could not delegate their rights even to their own children. Transfers of authority or surrender of territory being thus legally impossible, Irish 'acts of submission' were in no way binding on the clan or on any new chief elected by the clan.

In 1547 Edward VI succeeded his father. During his short reign, two English Lord Deputies in Ireland, Sir Edward Bellingham and Sir Anthony St. Leger, were able to make official boasts of organized killings of large numbers of the Irish. But Edward's counsellors regarded these reports as an inadequate return for the expensive efforts to suppress the now almost incessant insurrection. To the people of England, Ireland continued to be a liability rather than an asset; and to England's rulers it could be made to provide real money only by selling bits of it to unsuspecting Englishmen.

THE PLANTATION POLICY

The accession to the English throne of Edward's half-sister, Mary, an ardent Catholic, was hailed with relief by the still mainly Catholic Irish people. But her inauguration of the new 'Plantation Policy' in Ireland — a policy which had been earlier proposed to Henry VIII and rejected by him as too barbarous — quickly disillusioned them.

Mary began by confiscating the patrimony of the O'Moores in Leix and the O'Connors in Offaly. The former she renamed 'Queen's County' in honour of herself; the latter was renamed 'King's County' in honour of her Spanish husband. Her efforts to 'plant' the confiscated territory with new settlers from England had only a temporary success. The Irish clans stubbornly refused to be dispossessed without a struggle. With Rory O'Moore at their head, they overran the English settlements, time after time, 'like furies of hell with flakes of fire on poles'. And when Rory was captured, in 1578, the fight was carried on by his equally celebrated son, Owen.

Stung by official jibes at his failure, the English deputy at last invited most of the chief men of the O'Moores and O'Connors to a peace conference at Mullaghmast and there had them massacred. Their wives and children he hanged. Even then the 'planted' English did not find peace. Survivors of the dispossessed Irish, driven into the fastness of mountain and bog, banded themselves together and waged a new kind of war against the invaders. Today it would be called guerrilla warfare and the men who waged it came to be known as 'Tories', an anglicized derivative of the Irish word *toraidhe,* meaning 'a pursuer'.

Queen Elizabeth, on her accession to the English throne, attempted to extend the 'Plantation Policy' into Ulster. She made grants in counties Down and Antrim to Englishmen of her own choice, leaving it to them to dispossess the Irish and hold the land on behalf of the Crown. When they failed she made a grant of nearly the whole of County Antrim to Water Devereux, 8th Earl of Essex, and also provided money to cover the cost of its occupation. But Irish resistance soon disheartened the men who had gone with Essex in the hope of making quick fortunes. In desperation, Essex offered to make peace with the local Irish chief, Brian O'Neill. Having then been invited to a banquet, in O'Neill's stronghold, Essex there had his escort seize his host and hostess and put to the sword all the members of O'Neill's household, some 'two hundred men, women, youths and maidens'. English law, with the help of English garrisons, was now being enforced in several Ulster towns and Essex therefore had O'Neill and his wife publicly executed as traitors. He then opened negotiations with MacDonnell of Antrim and while temporizing with the latter and his chiefs, about a supposed parley, sent one of his captains and a force of 300 English soldiers to Rathlin Island, MacDonnell's stronghold, where they massacred the women, the children and the sick and wounded who had been gathered there for greater safety. In revenge for these outrages Brian O'Neill's son captured Belfast Castle and put the entire English garrison to the sword. MacDonnell similarly wiped out an English garrison at Carrickfergus. That put an end to the second 'plantation' of Ulster. After trying in vain to sell his concession, Essex departed.

SCORCHED EARTH

Ten years later, in 1585, Queen Elizabeth essayed an official State 'plantation' of Munster. There, acting on a suggestion made by Edmund Spenser, author of the 'Faerie Queen', the English Lord Deputy had already experimented with a 'scorched-earth' policy. As evidence of his success, contemporary English chroniclers were able to report that there was not to be heard the lowing of a single cow from the Rock of Cashel to the sea, that dead humans lay by every wayside and that such survivors as had been observed were 'mere anatomies of death', no longer able to walk, yet trying to crawl on hands and knees to search for edible weeds. But once again the resilience of the Irish people triumphed. An official investigation in 1592 showed that the Munster 'plantation' had been reduced to a mere 277 families. In the succeeding generation the survivors married with the Irish, adopted the language and customs of the country and became a part of the Irish nation.

An attempted 'plantation' of Connacht met with rather more success. There it had been preceded by massacres and enforced starvations which had provoked, even 'submitted' chiefs into revolt and the failure of the revolt had left Connacht temporarily broken and bleeding.

In 1593, Ulster came suddenly alive, Maguire, Chief of Fermanagh, stung by the outrages of English officials, rose in revolt and, having defeated an English army sent against him, attacked and captured Enniskillen.

But all these events were but a few of the incidental preliminaries to a period of complicated and confusing history in which the fortunes of the Irish nation steadily deteriorated; a period, however, made notable by the exploits of Hugh O'Neill — his victory over Queen's Marshall Bagnel at the Battle of the Yellow Ford and his later victory over Robert Devereux, 9th Earl of Essex. It is illuminated by the brave endeavours of Hugh O'Donnell and his intrepid 'Kernes' and by the famous fighting retreat of O'Sullivan Beare from Glengarriff to Leitrim. But it is darkened by the fateful defeat of the Irish at Kinsale and by the subsequent flight of the Earls O'Neill and O'Donnell to the continent of Europe which left Ireland largely leaderless in the hour of her greatest need.

THE THIRD PLANTATION OF ULSTER

In England, James I had succeeded Elizabeth and among the early decisions of the new king's counsellors had been one intended finally to subdue the troublesome Irish in the North. Six of Ulster's nine counties, Donegal, Derry, Armgh, Tyrone, Fermanagh and Cavan, were now declared forfeit to the Crown and large tracts of the confiscated land were assigned for occupation by undertakers from Britain or sold to London City Guilds. The less fertile areas of the seized land were allocated in smaller holdings to English 'servitors' and one-tenth of the whole was assigned to the dispossessed Irish. The historic Ulster (Ulaidh) of the Heptarchy — approximately equal to the present counties of Antrim and Down — was not 'planted'.

The third 'plantation of Ulster' began inauspiciously. To find the required number of settlers it had been necessary to recruit bankrupt shopkeepers, insolvent debtors, and released convicts. A contemporary chronicler of their own (the Rev. Ambrose Stewart) describes the new settlers as 'scum' — men whose 'carriage made them to be abhorred at home'. But the rightful owners of the confiscated land, resorting once again to 'tory-war',, quickly thinned out the new arrivals. Though said to have numbered originally 8,000, the recognizably 'planted' families in Ulster had, by 1622, been considereably reduced. The refusal of the rightful owners of the land to submit meekly made the tenancies of many of settlers altogether undesirable; those who were able to return home counted themselves among the fortunate. Others, particularly the Gaelic-speaking settlers from Scotland, who shared a common ancestry, a common language and common traditions with the native Irish, openly ignored the restrictions of English law and, by intermarriage and the adoption of Irish ways, made common cause with the Irish. Today, the six Ulster counties which comprise British-occupied 'Northern Ireland' include only four of the 'planted' counties. Two of those four now have Nationalist majorities and, within the rest of the British-occupied area, not more than a hundred recognizably 'planter' surnames have survived.

IRELAND RISES AGAIN

The parliament of Charles I saw Ireland only as a potential source of revenue. Confiscated lands were sold and re-sold and sold again. The Poynings' Laws were reinforced by penal enactments against Roman Catholics. And so far as English law could enforce its own prohibition, the Irish were deprived of enough of the means of livelihood to permit English officials to congratulate themselves that the conquest of Ireland had been at last completed. But in 1641 Ireland rose again. In the Midlands a lead was given by the O'Moore of Leix, a chief of the clan which Queen Mary had tried to exterminate eighty-five years earlier. In Ulster, the real head was Phelim O'Neill. In North Leinster, it opened with a defeat of the English army at Drogheda and the consequent winning over of prominent Catholic noblemen of the English Pale. To suppress this rising, the English Parliament voted a sum of £1,000,000 to be raised by re-confiscating already confiscated land in Ireland and re-selling it to more unsuspecting English adventurers. This desperate swindle found but few victims.

In Ulster, where the worst outrages against the Irish were of recent memory, the rising spread rapidly. It was, in part, a renewal of the 'tory-war' against the English 'planters' of whom a possible 3,000 were killed. But even in Ulster, acts of violence against life and property were a feature only of the early unorganized stages of the insurrection. As it got under way and was better organised, plundering and the harrassing of non-combatants were severely punished and even captured enemy garrisons were allowed to go free to fight again. This leniency was neither appreciated nor helpful. But on the other side, the butchering of the Irish peasantry, without regard to age or sex, and the indiscriminate destruction of property by the English government forces caused many more of the Norman-Irish and the Anglo-Irish to join the insurgents. This accession of strength made it possible to set up an Irish government or 'confederation' at Kilkenny; and military success soon made the Kilkenny Confederation the only effective government in three-quarters of the country.

THE PARLIAMENTARIANS

The break between King Charles and his Parliament, however, found echoes among the Irish 'Confederates'. There were those who fought for 'King and Covenant', those who fought only for freedom of worship as Roman Catholics and those who fought for both national and religious freedom.

In the course of the insurrection England had raised a Scottish army for service in Ireland. This army now changed its allegiance from King to Parliament and Charles was forced in his own interests to conciliate the Irish insurgents with an offer of freedom of religion. This won over many of the Confederates and, as a result of the change in policy, the greatest of the Irish military leaders, Eoghan Roe O'Neill, eventually found himself waging war against the Parliamentarians on behalf of the English king. He won a brilliant victory at Benburb, in Ulster, and in the course of the following year he and other Irish leaders achieved further triumphs. But the divergent loyalties and the dissentions and jealousies which were growing more and more acute within the Confederation soon left Ireland once again without effective leadership. And in 1649 the English king, Charles I, on whose behalf Ireland's newly-won strength had been dissipated, was executed at Whitehall by his own people.

CROMWELL

In that same year, Oliver Cromwell, who had been appointed Lord Lieutenant of Ireland by the English Parliament, landed in Dublin and there began a new era of violence, bloodshed and stark cruelty against which the naked valour of the Irish people was of little avail. By the end of the Cromwellian war the total population of Ireland had been reduced to less than a million. Some 600,000 Irish and Anglo-Irish had been massacred, starved to death or killed in battle and some thousands of Irish women and children — mostly the widows and orphans of the liquidated landowners — had been shipped off to the West Indies to be sold as slaves.

Cromwell's war of revenge also brought in its wake further confiscations and further ambitious attempts to reduce the Irish people to savagery and to eeradicate all memory of a national past. Bards and scholars and craftsmen were hunted down and hanged, schools were scattered, trade and industry were systematically suppressed, Irish books were burned, gems of the craftsmen's art were pillaged or destroyed and all Irish learning was made impossible.

Back in Queen Elizabeth's time, the ill-fated Earl of Essex had informed his queen that the Irish 'were so framed to be soldiers' that he feared that the war would be 'great and costly and long'; that though he did 'unwillingly confess it' they had 'better bodies and perfecter use of their arms' than the men her Majesty was sending over. And, as a propagandist, Essex offered a piece of advice: ' 'Twere as well for our credit,' he wrote, 'that we had the exposition of our quarrel with this people, and not they with us.'

Cromwell, like other would-be conquerors before and

after him, endeavoured to follow that advice. The Irish were therefore robbed of food for bodies, minds and souls so that barbarous pictures of Irish life and Irish character might pass unchallenged in the guise of history. But the end was not yet.

JAMES AND WILLIAM

Like the accession of Queen Mary, the return to power of King Charles II brought new hope to Ireland but once again Ireland participated in the changed course of events mainly as a victim. And when Charles II was followed by James II, an avowed Catholic, there were new and stronger hopes of justice for Ireland.

Among the English settlers in Ireland, now augmented by some of Cromwell's officers and men, the change produced something of a panic and the appointment of Talbot, Earl of Tyrconnel, as Lord Deputy started a general exodus from Ireland of such English settlers and Parliamentarians as could muster the means to remove themselves. But in England, James was soon faced with disloyalty in his army and Tyrconnel was obliged to send some of his own troops to the king's assistance. In spite of his precarious position at home, James initiated some half-hearted attempts to restore confiscated lands in Ireland and otherwise to do justice to the oppressed Irish majority. It was for these reasons that, having been forced to flee from England, he looked to Ireland for salvation.

In 1689, he landed at Kinsale on the south coast of Ireland bringing with him some French military aid, and uniforms, arms and ammunition for the equipping of Irish levies.

In the meantime, the throne of England had been offered to Mary, the Protestant daughter of the Catholic James II, co-jointly with her Dutch husband, William of

Orange; and the dispossessed Irish now found themselves involved in a war on behalf of the dispossessed English king.

Most of the remaining English settlers in the North, and some of the English regiments in that area, had already switched their loyalty from English James to Dutch William. The Earl of Tyrconnel, as James's Lord Deputy, had therefore planned to replace the mutinous English garrison in Derry by the still-loyal regiment of Lord Antrim. The English authorities in the city decided on surrender but a few local apprentice boys took it upon themselves to shut the gates of the city and popular apprehension then forced the authorities to refuse admission to the loyalist forces.

Five weeks after James's landing at Kinsale a Jacobite army began a siege of Derry. It was a comparatively small army with little or no artillery and without the necessary ordnance, medical and supply services. But for 105 days, the considerably more numerous and better equipped disloyalists within the strongly walled city remained on the defensive, making no effective sortie and declining all offers of free pardon and full religious and civic rights. The arrival of more mutinous English regiments and some long-delayed supply ships eventually compelled the Jacobite army to abandon the siege.

In the following month a Dutch general, Schomberg, landed in the North with some 15,000 further reinforcements. He captured Carrickfergus and moved on Dundalk. But, within three months, he had lost half his men and was obliged to appeal to William for still more reinforcements.

James's forces had also been much depleted but, having appealed to France, he secured 7,000 well-trained French troops. In exchange he caused to be shipped to France an almost equal number of Irish levies to be trained as soldiers for the army of King Louis.

William headed his reinforcements himself. Like Schomberg, he landed at Carrickfergus and moved on to Dundalk. His union with Schomberg brought the Williamite forces up to approximately 35,000 men, well-armed and well-equipped. In addition to William's own Dutch troops, the Williamite force included eight regiments of German mercenaries, the Danish Royal Guards and some French Huguenots. It also included the remnants of the disloyal English regiments and a couple of regiments recruited locally from English settlers and nationally apostate Irish. For its martial music, William's army had a token force of drummers from the Papal Guard of the Vatican.

The Jacobite forces, not more than 25,000 strong, were made up of loyal English regiments, the French reinforcements, some Irish cavalry and some largely untrained Irish infantry.

Having unwisely abandoned the security of Dublin, James advanced northwards and met the Williamite forces at the River Boyne. The battle which ensued was described by a contemporary French chronicler as 'a mere cavalry skirmish'. But, though the gallantry of the Irish cavalry in this 'skirmish' excited the admiration of their opponents, James's preoccupation with his own safety and his consequent withdrawal of some of his best regiments and all but six small pieces of his artillery, to protect his own person, gave the decision to William.

James fled to France but his army re-organized and retreated towards the Shannon. Still loyal to James and still obediently fighting under the command of leaders appointed by James – leaders who neither knew Ireland nor local conditions of warfare – the Jacobite army lost further battles at Athlone and Aughrim. But then came Limerick, where Patrick Sarsfield, by his spectacular destruction of the Williamite siege train at Ballyneety and by his inspiring leadership of the Irish citizens and of the remnants of the Jacobite army in Limerick, so wore down the enemy in two battles that William was forced finally to make terms.

The Irish success at Limerick won from William a guarantee of religious freedom and the restoration of Irish rights. But it procured for William the demobilization of Sarsfield's army and, when that had been achieved, the important clauses of the Treaty were repudiated by William's English Parliament.

From that broken Treaty of Limerick sprang the Irish brigades of other armies, recruited from exiled officers and men who entered the service of France, Spain and other Continental powers.

THE PENAL LAWS

By means of Penal Laws passed during the reigns of William III and his successors, Anne and George II, the Irish at home who declined to be made 'English' were condemned to poverty, ignorance and economic serfdom. And so far as English domination in Ireland was concerned these penal laws — described by Edmund Burke as 'an elaborate contrivance for the oppression, impoverishment and degradation of a people and the debasement in them of human nature itself' — achieved a measure of success. Between 1703 and 1788, countless Roman Catholic land-owners changed their religion, largely anglicized their names and gained propserity and protection as a part of the Protestant 'ascendancy'. High posts in Church and State, however, continued to be filled by Englishmen. And while the landlords grew rich and tyrannical, their tenants — both Catholics and 'Dissenters' — sank into serfdom; and the the great mass of the landless Irish were forced further and further into that hopelessness of poverty and despair which so aroused the indignation of Dean Swift. Homeless refugees now roamed the countryside; scores of thousands died of starvation; and more than a million others abandoned the struggle and emigrated to the North American Colonies. Among the latter were the volunteer Protestant defenders of Derry who, betrayed by those they had served, emigrated *en masse* to America, and there founded Londonderry, New Hampshire.

IRELAND OVERSEAS

In America's subsequent struggle for independence a large number of Washington's soldiers and officers, including thirty-nine of his generals, were of Irish birth or Irish parentage. And fighting for Washington against the English, as a part of that Irish section, were the grandsons of the betrayed defenders of Derry.

In Ireland, the old Gaelic civilization was now a part of an almost vanished past. But there still remained scholars whose lives were devoted to keeping Irish learning alive and there were still poets to stir the memory of the past and kindle and re-kindle hopes of a new national future. It was due to those men, to the 'hedge-school masters' and to the outlawed bards that the English conquest of Ireland remained incomplete. About this time, also, there began the long chain of secret and sometimes semi-military Irish organizations which were to make the English conquest of Ireland forever impossible of completion. And, by a strange irony, England in the days of her greatest danger was heavily dependent on Irishmen to save herself from conquest. As early as 1770, according to Lord Charles Beresford (in his *Nelson and his Times*), there were 'English men-of-war in which nearly the whole crews were composed of Irishmen who would scarcely speak one word of English'.

Early in 1778 France allied herself with the rebel colonists of North American and her ships were threatening
the coasts of Ireland and Britain. The inadequacy of the
British forces in Ireland to meet a possible invasion
forced the British administration to permit its subordinate Irish Parliament to raise a Volunteer Force. But
contrary to official anticipation, the Volunteers pre-
ferred to give their attention to domestic questions and,
in 1779, their threat of armed intervention resulted in
some easing of the penal discrimination against
Catholics and the removal of some of the restrictions on
Irish trade. They were also mainly responsible for the
passing of the Act of 1782 giving to the Irish Parliament a
legislative independence which, in the words of the Act,
'should at no future time be questioned or question-
able'. The fruits of this new legislative independence were
quickly apparent in an amazing national recovery.
'Ireland', wrote Sir Jonah Barrington, 'rose in wealth, in
trade, in manufactures, in agriculture and every branch
of industry that could enhance her value or render a
people rich and prosperous.' Land confiscation ceased
and Relief Bills abolished Catholic disabilities in regard
to land tenure and inheritance, the restriction in regard
to residence imposed on Catholic priests and the law
which had hitherto forbidden Catholics to teach.

But the English-controlled Administration in Ireland
was not answerable to the Irish Parliament and, with or
without legislative independence, the Irish Parliament
was by no means a truly representative body. Its members were exclusively Protestant and, though they
included good patriots, they also included corrupt place-
seekers without ideals and often without principles. The
profits of the new order therefore reached only those
who were least in need. To remedy some of the worst of

33

the remaining evils, the Irish Volunteers next endeavoured to secure certain Parliamentary reforms. But in this they were out-manoeuvred and shortly afterwards they allowed themselves to be disbanded, thus leaving the vast majority of the population of Ireland again helpless, still living in poverty and still suffering under both religious and civil disabilities. Some of these disabilities had for some time been shared by the Presbyterians of Ulster and by non-Conformists generally throughout Ireland; for they, while mainly subservient to English rule in Ireland, declined to acknowledge the authority of the English king in religious matters.

Like the Roman Catholics, these Dissenters had also to pay tithes to the Established (Episcopalian) Church. And the double scourge of 'law' and landlords and the deliberate suppression in Ireland of every industry deemed likely to endanger England's own commerical prosperity, drove more and more Ulster Presbyterians into exile or sowed the seeds of revolt among those who remained.

Differences of religion, as such, were no longer the real reason for political discrimination. They served as an excuse for plunder and as a means of preserving the divisions and dissensions which were a feature of English rule in Ireland. And though it suited the Administration to pretend otherwise, differences of religion had little or no relation to racial distinctions. The Protestant 'Ascendancy' now had a considerable leavening of the real Irish, the Presbyterians of the North were largely the descendants of the Irish who had colonized Scotland centuries before, while among the impoverished Catholic peasantry of the South there were descendants of Elizabethan and Cromwellian 'planters' and many whose names could have been found on that exclusive patent of Norman nobility, the Battle Roll of Hastings.

In 1790 Theobald Wolfe Tone, Henry Joy MacCracken, Thomas Russell and a few other liberal-minded Protestants, stirred by the fall of the Bastille in France, began to advocate a re-union of Irishmen of every religious persuasion for the purpose of establishing in Ireland a social order 'founded on the principles of civil, political and religious liberty'. The result was the establishment in Belfast of the 'Society of United Irishmen'. The English administration now made an attempt to enlist the influence of the Church of Rome in opposing the spread of French revolutionary doctrines; and new Catholic Relief Bills admitted Catholics to the Parliamentary and municipal franchise, gave legal validity to marriages of Protestants with Catholics, permitted Catholics to carry arms, to hold commissions in the navy and army, to qualify for University degrees, to enter the learned professions and to sit on juries. But the retention of a 'test oath', repugnant to Catholics, still debarred them from taking effective part in the government of their own country. And, to avoid the threatened danger of a union of Catholics and Protestants, the concessions granted were soon made an excuse for stirring up a new and bitter spirit of intolerance. In the North, this took concrete form in the establishment of the 'Peep o' Day Boys' and other secret organizations of lower-grade Protestants which had for their purpose the expulsion of Roman Catholics from their homes. In 1795 there was a revival of the Orange Society in which some of the most bigoted of the lower-class Protestants banded themselves together as 'lodges' and, aided by the government, inaugurated their own 'reign of terror'. The Catholics countered with another secret organization, the 'Defenders', and in 1796 the government armed the Orangemen and created 'Yeomanry Regiments' for a flagrantly one-sided suppression of ,'disorders'. The excesses of which these 'Yeomen' were guilty had the effect of enlisting sympathy and support for Roman Catholics among many respectable Protestants, including both Presbyterian and Episcopalian clergymen, and the Society of United Irishmen grew rapidly in strength. Wolfe Tone then went to France to seek aid for a straightforward effort 'to break the connection with England, the never-failing source of all our political evils'. The response was generous but the first French invasion fleet was scattered by a storm and a second one arrived too late. For, in the meantime, the outrages against Roman Catholics and Dissenters had provoked the United Irishmen into premature revolt.

There were initial Irish successes in Ulster and Wexford. But the English threw in reinforcements of regular English regiments, Militia Regiments of local riff-raff — Catholic and Protestant — and German Mercenaries known as 'Hessians'. And the Irish Republic, proclaimed in Belfast so short a while before, suffered an eclipse which was to last until our own generation. Most of the leaders of the United Irishmen, Protestant and Catholic, clergymen and laymen alike, perished on the scaffold or died in English prisons. But their protest had not been altogether in vain. With the increased legislative powers won from England and the new ideals acquired from the United Irishmen the nation made so amazing a recovery that by the end of the eighteenth century it had become more than ever a threat to England's commercial supremacy. The Irish Parliament was therefore abolished.

The disastrous effects of the new legislative union with England soon provoked a new insurrection, this time led by a young Protestant, Robert Emmet. It failed ingloriously but it made the name of its gallant leader an inspiration to every generation which followed him.

During the first forty years of Ireland's new status as a part of the 'United Kingdom of Great Britain and Ireland', the various British governments suspended the Habeas Corpus Act in Ireland nineteen times, passed seventeen Coercion Acts, ten Insurrection and Arms Acts and two Unlawful Oaths Acts.

During the same period, hundreds of thousands of Irishmen, particularly those who might have proved an obstacle to the degradation of the Nation, were impressed into the British armed forces. In 1803 Irish soldiers were praised in the British House of Commons for having played an important and honourable part in driving Napoleon's army out of Egypt and Irish sailors serving in the British Navy were thanked for having merited 'the great indebtedness' of Nelson for his victories at sea. And after the Battle of Waterloo the Duke of Wellington told the British House of Lords: 'It is mainly to the Catholic Irish that we owe all our predominance in our military career and that I personally am indebted for the laurels with which you have been pleased to decorate my brow.' He further assured the Lords that 'no victory could have been obtained without the blood and valour of the Catholic Irish'. These statements were made by Wellington in the course of his successful appeal to the House of Lords to pass the final Catholic Relief Bill which, by abolishing the 'Test Oath', at last permitted Roman Catholics to hold offices of State and seats in Parliament.

THE FAMINE

The passing of that Bill put an end to Daniel O'Connell's twenty-five years of agitation for 'Catholic Emancipation' and he then began a similar agitation for a repeal of the 'Act of Union'.

A revolt against the pacifist teachings of O'Connell

37

had already led John Mitchel, together with Gavan Duffy, William Smith O'Brien, Devin Reilly and other 'Young Irelanders', to establish the 'Irish Confederation'.

Mitchel's continued appeals to the Irish farmers, Catholic and Protestant alike, to oppose the seizure of their crops was too much of a challenge to the British administration. John Mitchel was seized, charged with the newly-invented crime of 'treason-felony' and transported overseas. His task then fell to John Martin — who, like Mitchel, was an Ulster Protestant — but he too was seized and transported. Meagher, O'Brien and other leaders of the Irish Confederation, convinced that an insurrection just then could only end in failure, bided their time. But before that time arrived, the multitude on whom they had counted were wallowing in straw on workhouse floors. To a 'workhouse fever' there was now added a 'workhouse ophthalmia' and a 'workhouse dysentery'. And the children of the new generation were growing up physically and mentally crippled because of deficiencies in nourishment.

Police and soldiers were now everywhere — enforcing the latest Coercion Act, searching for hidden weapons, ejecting tenants, pulling down houses and escorting cattle and produce to the ports as though carrying out raids in an enemy country. In 1848 another suspension of the Habeas Corpus Act, and the issue of warrants, forced the Irish Confederation into a premature rising. It lasted only a few hours and its leaders followed Mitchel and Martin into enforced exile. 'Now,' said *The London Times,* 'for the first time these six hundred years, England has Ireland at her mercy, and can deal with her as she pleases.'

The Times was wrong. Eight years later, O'Donovan Rossa founded the 'Phoenix Club' in County Cork. Under the influence of James Stephens — who had escaped arrest after participating in the short-lived '48 rising — this developed into a secret society which, in its turn, served as a foundation for the Fenian Brotherhood (a name adopted by its founder John O'Mahoney from that of the Fianna, a third-century Irish chivalric brotherhood). By 1860 the Fenian movement had acquired considerable strength in the United States of American and in that same year *The London Times* issued a 'Fenian warning' to its English readers. 'America,' it said, 'is much more Irish than the English people are apt to conceive. The great majority of the white population there is of Irish descent and it is the Irish element that has long governed the politics of the United States.'

But the next year the American Civil War broke out and some 175,000 Irishmen — many of them Fenians — fought in the Federal Army while other thousands, including three sons of John Mitchel, fought for the Southerns. In spite of this set-back, the Fenians at home eventually decided on a rising; but, as before, the Government was forewarned and forearmed. There were skirmishes at several places throughout Ireland, none of which achieved more than temporary success. But the aftermath of the failure was something not foreseen by the Government. Though executions were few, many hundreds of Fenians were sentenced to savage terms of imprisonment and in the general reaction the movement acquired new life as the Irish Republican Brotherhood, the most successful of all Ireland's secret military organizations.

Charles James Fox, British statesman and orator, once described the Act of Union which had come into force in 1801 as 'atrocious in its principles and abominable in its means'. Of the government of Ireland after the passing of the Act, Grattan said: 'To find a worse government . . . you must go to Hell for your policy and Bedlam for your methods.' Gladstone, nearly a century later, said of the Act that he knew of 'no blacker or fouler transaction in the history of man'. The historian Lecky described it as having been 'extorted by the most enormous corruption in the history of representative institutions.' Yet now there was in Ireland a 'Unionist Party' that took its name and its political creed from the Act which Lecky further described as 'a crime of deepest turpitude'. The Presbyterians of Ulster, seduced by the subsidizing of their clergy; the Orangemen, incited by fears of re-tribution; the rich Ulster merchants and linen lords, bribed with the promise of cheap labour and the big land-owners, made selfish by the assurance of undis-turbed possession of stolen estates, had joined forces with the hordes of English officials, with both Protestant and Catholic placehunters, with what John Mitchel was later to call 'the Lord Lieutenant's lion-and-unicorn tradesmen' and with recently-arrived English com-mercial adventurers, to make up the political party which, right down to our own generation, has resisted all progressive statutes, made itself the main obstacle to national independence and still constitutes the main obstacle to national unity in Ireland.

But the enforced decline of Irish agriculture was now bankrupting farmers and inducing the landlords to devote more and more of their land to pasture. Between 1841 and 1851, half the small-holders of Ireland had been evicted to make room for cattle and sheep. Then came some undoing of the confiscations for landlords squandered their revenues and fell into debt. And an 'Encumbered Estates Act' authorized the compulsory sale of debt-encumbered properties. This, in its turn, led to some badly-needed land reform legislation.

HOME RULE

Home Rule agitation and the activities of the Land League occupied the minds of Irishmen of the next generation and for a while 'The Irish Question' became the shuttlecock of British politics, for Irish members of the British Parliament now occasionally held the balance of power.

At any time during this period the granting of 'Home Rule' — even with the limited powers claimed for it — might have satisfied Ireland's aspirations. But it took the eclipse of the moderate Isaac Butt, the activities of spasmodic 'resistance movements' in the 'land war' at home, the growth of democratic understanding among the English working-classes, the practical manifestations of sympathy with Ireland's cause in America, the organizing abilities of Michael Davitt, the invention of the 'boycott' and the obstructionist tactics of Joseph Biggar and Parnell in the British House of Commons to persuade the British Government to lend a favourable ear to Ireland's demands.

In 1893 Gladstone forced a Home Rule Bill through the British House of Commons but it was defeated in the House of Lords. In 1912 another Home Rule Bill was passed in the Commons and, owing to recent limitations of the powers of the House of Lords, there was now every possibility of the Bill becoming law. But, in Ireland the 'Unionists' met the threat to their vested interests with a new appeal to the sectarian passions of the rank and file of their supporters. For their protagonist they chose a man described by Mr. St. John Ervine as 'the last stage-Irishman' — Edward Carson, the Dublin-born grandson of an Italian named Carsoni. Three months later the Orange mobs of Belfast began a terror-drive against Roman Catholics. In the same year there was created the 'Ulster Volunteers', flamboyantly pledged to resist the Home Rule threat to prescriptive Orange rights and privileges. Arms were secured from Germany and in 1913 — the Ulster 'loyalists' having changed their 'loyalty' once again — Carson was sent to Germany to open negotiations with the Kaiser.

THE IRISH VOLUNTEERS

The Irish Republican Brotherhood which, throughout a generation of political agitation, had continued to prepare in its own way for the struggle for Irish independence, now decided to counter Carson's move by creating a Nationalist armed force and, on 25 November 1913, there was launched the Irish Volunteers.

In Dublin there had been a general 'lock-out' of twenty-four thousand workers. Protest meetings organized by the Irish Labour Party had been broken up by the police. Two unarmed men and one woman had been killed and scores of others injured and the chief labour organizer, James Larkin, had been imprisoned for 'using seditious language'.

One month after the outbreak of that first World War the Home Rule Bill became law, only to be followed by a dishonest amending act which suspended its operation for the duration of the war. To many in Ireland the amending act made the Home Rule Bill just 'another scrap of paper'; to others it was impossible for acceptance because of implied intentions to cut off most of Ulster from the rest of Ireland. But others, including Irish Parliamentary representatives and many of the Irish

Volunteers, failed to appreciate its weaknesses and now favoured Ireland's participation in 'the war for democracy'. The result was a split in the Nationalist forces and, in the course of the next four years, approximately 200,000 young men from Ireland joined the army and navy of Britain while, even before the intorduction of conscription in Britain itself, 115,000 Irishmen resident in that country had similarly volunteered their services.

THE EASTER RISING

Undeterred by the sudden weakening of the Nationalist forces by the 1914 war, the Irish Republican Brotherhood continued to organize the nation for a continuance of the struggle.

'This aged people,' wrote Patrick Pearse, 'has renewed its youth ... we are young today as men were young when to be a young man was to be a hero.'

On Easter Monday, 24 April 1916, the Irish Volunteers and the Citizen Army seized strategic points in Dublin and proclaimed an Irish Republic. 'In every generation,' stated that proclamation, 'the Irish people have asserted their right to national freedom.' In that one sentence was summed up seven and a half centuries of Ireland's struggle against world-be conquerors.

But the 1916 insurrection ended after a week of gallant fighting against overhwelming odds. Fifteen of the leaders were executed within a few days of their surrender and some two thousand were imprisoned. 'The shot Irishmen,' wrote George Bernard Shaw' 'will now take their places beside Robert Emmet and the Manchester Martyrs in Ireland, and beside the heroes of Poland and Serbia and Belgium in Europe; and nothing in Heaven or earth can prevent it ...'

Shaw was proved to be right. The executions served to

awaken in the people of Ireland a new sense of national pride, a pride which was further developed in a re-awakening of interest in Ireland's historic past. And while the first World War dragged on, Ireland, helped by her friends in America, reorganized and rebuilt to such good effect that, at the General Election of 1919, no less than seventy-three Republicans and six Parliamentary 'Home Rulers' were elected out of a total of one hundred and five. Among the former was Constance Gore-Booth (Countess Markiewicz), the first woman ever to be elected a Member of Parliament.

Britain's unforgivable sin — the proposed partitioning of the oldest historic nation in Western Europe and the most geographically complete entity in the world — had already earned the condemnations of Catholic and Protestant bishops and of Catholic and Protestant writers. And now the great mass of the plain people of Ireland had pronounced judgement on it.

THE FIRST DÁIL

With the result of the general election as their mandate, those of the newly-elected Republican candidates who were not in prison or in exile met in Dublin on 21 January 1919, issued a declaration of independence and established Dáil Eireann, a Republican Government and legislature, with Mr. Eamon de Valera as its President. The Irish Volunteers who, in spite of more imprisonments and more executions, had resumed the unfinished fight then became the Irish Republican Army.

British government in Ireland had always been without legality. The establishment of Dáil Eireann, as an independent parliament for all Ireland, now made it doubly illegal. For the men who constituted Dáil Eireann had been elected in accordance with British electoral law and they spoke for the overwhelming majority of the

44

Irish people. Soon they received from the people a still more emphatic mandate; in the all-Ireland elections for local government bodies, held in 1919 and 1920, Republican candidates secured ninety-one per cent of the total poll.

The British Government replied with fulminations and martial law. And since neither British regular soldiers nor the still mainly Irish 'Constabulary' could safely be asked to put into execution the new British Government plants, it was decided to recruit in England a modern equivalent of the 'Yeomanry' of earlier repressions. From the mixture of army khaki and almost black police uniforms issued to these 'ten-shillings-a-day-mercenaries', they came to be known as 'Black-and-Tans'.

In the course of the first year of their presence in Ireland the Black and Tans raided thousands of houses, burned ninety Irish towns and generally indulged in a profitable campaign of unrestrained pillage. And by the systematic murder of leaders of opinion — clergymen, teachers and public representatives — by the organized destruction of factories, creameries and other essential features of Ireland's economy, the motley horde of Britain's 'Crown Forces' tried once again to reduce Ireland to servility. Among early victims was Thomas MacCurtain, the first Republican Lord Mayor of Cork, who was shot in his own house. His successor, Terence MacSwiney, author of *Principles of Freedom,* was arrested, tried by court martial on a charge of being in possession of 'documents likely to cause disaffection to his Majesty' and died in an English prison after a hunger-strike which lasted for 73 days. No single event in all those eventful years so aroused world sympathy with Ireland's cause as the martyrdom of MacSwiney.

The greatest blow to British prestige during this period was the complete breakdown of her civil administration in Ireland. Almost all local government was now under the jurisdiction of Dáil Eireann. British officials could not collect taxes, British courts had been supplanted by Republican, or Sinn Fein, courts and Ireland had sent its own Republican envoys to Washington, Paris, Rome and Madrid.

THE GOVERNMENT OF IRELAND ACT

Harassed still further by military defeats which had necessitated the withdrawal of outlying garrisons and badgered by British big business which was losing its foreign markets because of an increasingly hostile world opinion, Britain, in November 1920, passed a new Government of Ireland Act. This time, it was proposed to establish two separate puppet parliaments in Ireland – one in Belfast for the six counties of North-East Ulster and one in Dublin for the remaining twenty-six counties. Both parliaments were to have the same limited powers of local autonomy and, by thus arbitrarily dividing the National economy, it was believed that Ireland could not become the dangerous commercial rival which she had threatened to become before the Act of Union destroyed her previous Parliament.

In the British Parliament the new Partition Act came nominally into force on 3 May 1921 and the elections of members to the two parliaments were fixed for later in the same month. By the provisions of this exclusively British Act – the move had no mandate from any section of the Irish people – the twenty-six counties of Ireland – which included Donegal, the most northerly county of all – were to be known as 'Southern Ireland', while the six counties in the north-east of Ulster were to be known as 'Northern Ireland'. The Act allocated 128 seats to the Parliament for the twenty-six counties and 52 to that for the six counties.

The Republican Government, while denying Britain's

right to determine the destiny of Ireland, decided to utilize the proposed elections as a new demonstration of the will of the Irish people. It was decreed that the elected candidates would constitute the Second Dáil Eireann.

Because of the general detestation of the whole idea of 'partition', there were no contests in the twenty-six county area; in every case a Republican candidate was returned unopposed. But four of the eight University seats, allotted on a special franchise, were won by non-Republicans.

In the meantime, during that year which saw the establishment of the Northern Ireland Parliament (1921), the war in the rest of Ireland was causing grave concern in Britain. It was not going according to plan.

The Irish forces in England's latest war against Ireland were incredibly small compared with those arrayed against them but they had an intelligence service, directed by Michael Collins, which was immeasurably superior to that of their enemies; it permeated the entire British administration and it was becoming almost impossible for the British forces to make a move without the advance knowledge of the Irish. Captured Vickers and Lewis guns, frequently handled by Irishmen who had learned their business in the first World War, were now making it possible to carry the war into the enemy camp, even to the extent of capturing and destroying British barracks, attacking troop-trains and raiding airfields; and in 1921, thanks to American aid, the Irish Republican Army was able to introduce to its opponents a new weapon at which the British professed to be shocked: the 'Tommy gun'.

DISGRACING THE NAME OF BRITAIN

Winston Churchill who, a few years earlier, had narrow-

47

ly escaped being lynched by a Belfast Orange mob for advocating 'Home Rule for Ireland' now advocated the recruiting in England — for the war in Ireland — of 'a hundred thousand new special troops and police' — to be equipped with 'thousands of armoured cars' and the 'lacing' of the three 'Southern Provinces' of Ireland with 'block-houses and barbed wire'. But, even in England, decent public opinion was already sickened and disgusted with the things being done by the British in Ireland — things which, in the words of *The London Times,* had 'lastingly disgraced the name of Britain'.

The jails were filled with Irish patriots but there was fighting on a larger scale. Four thousand persons, against whom there was no evidence and no means of formulating a charge, were held in British concentration camps but the 'whole British army was tethered to Ireland'. Martial law was proclaimed over a large portion of Ireland and 'official reprisals' and 'collective punishment' had been instituted but 'Britain's great interests in India and Egypt', and 'especially in the Dominions and the United States', were — Churchill admitted — being 'sensibly affected'.

And so, on 24 June 1921, the British Cabinet invited Mr. de Valera to a peace conference. The latter insisted on the cessation of hostilities as a preliminary to any discussion of terms and, on 11 July, both parties agreed to a truce.

UNEASY PEACE

Interviews between Mr. de Valera and the British Prime Minister (Lloyd George), and a subsequent exchange of notes, let to a decision by Mr. de Valera and his Cabinet to send a delegation to confer with members of the British Cabinet 'with a view to ascertaining how the association of Ireland with the community of nations known as the British Empire may best be reconciled with Irish national aspirations'. And, on 6 December, the Irish delegates put their signatures to a draft 'Articles of Agreement of a Treaty'. By this Treaty, Lloyd George later assured the British Parliament, Ireland would accept allegiance to the Crown, partnership in the British Empire and would 'subordinate her external relations to the judgment of the General Council.' Ireland would also accept a British-appointed Governor General with the right to veto any act of the Irish Parliament. The position of 'Northern Ireland' in the proposed new scheme of things remained ambiguous. Ireland — the whole of Ireland — was to become the 'Irish Free State' but the jurisdiction of the new State over the six partioned counties was to remain in abeyance for a period of one month; during that period, the Government of Northern Ireland was to have the right to 'opt out'; in which case a Boundary Commission was to be established for the purpose of ascertaining the wishes of the inhabitants and making territorial adjustments accordingly. The Irish delegates to the Peace Conference were assured — by their British co-signatories — that fair adjustments of territory in accordance with the wishes of the inhabitants would result in the return of the counties of Tyrone and Fermanagh, most of the counties of Derry and Armagh and the southern half of County Down, thus leaving the rest of the 'North' with little or no alternative to joining with the 'South'.

The Agreement also secured land, sea and air bases for Britain and committed Ireland to an acceptance of liability for the service of an unspecified proportion of the Public Debt of the United Kingdom and liability also for the payment of pensions (or compensation) to judges, civil service officials and police who, having served the British administration in Ireland, might be discharged or elect to resign in consequence of the change of government.

Mr. de Valera took the first possible opportunity publicly to repudiate the Agreement. But on 16 December, it came before the British Parliament and was there passed by an enthusiastic majority. In Dáil Eireann, many sound and convincing arguments were put forward both for and against its acceptance. Arthur Griffith, who had headed the peace delegation, expressed a sincere belief that it would lay the foundation of peace and friendship. By others it was argued that, having been signed under duress — as an alternative to Lloyd George's threatened 'immediate and terrible war' — it was without validity. Others counselled its acceptance as a 'stepping stone' — a policy which had the support of the Irish Republican Brotherhood. Mr. de Valera prophesised that its acceptance would split the country; his supporters, generally, insisted that a renewal of the war was preferable to a surrender to threats. But on 7 January 1922, the action of the Irish delegates in signing the Agreement was approved in the Second Dáil by sixty-four votes to fifty-seven.

Mr. de Valera resigned his Presidency. In accordance with the terms of the Agreement, a meeting was called of members of the already legally dead 'Parliament of Southern Ireland' and by them the Agreement was ratified as a Treaty. A Provisional Government was then established to implement its provisions.

Six months later, largely due to British insistence on a right to interfere in the actions of the Provisional Government and to dictate details of the new Irish Free State Constitution, a Civil War broke out between those who were prepared to work the Treaty and those who regarded its acceptance as a surrender. This tragic chapter in Ireland's history ended, in the summer of 1923, with a victory for the pro-Treaty forces. And the Government of the Irish Free State, with Mr. W. T. Cosgrave at its head, settled down to the difficult task of attempting to restore Ireland's economic life and her national culture.

On April 30, 1923, orders to halt the fighting were given by de Valera on behalf of the Republican Government. The Free State Government had by then taken prisoner and later interned, about ten thousand Republicans. During the war, a further seventy-seven had been executed. Among these latter was the author Erskine Childers, whose son, also named Erskine Childers, later became President of the Republic of Ireland. The war, however, also claimed many casualties on the Free State side. Among the fallen was the popular leader Michael Collins, still only 32, who had for a time held the office of Prime Minister.

De Valera was imprisoned and spent a year in jail. The civil war lasted a little less than a year, but hate and bitterness lingered in the minds of the participants. The Free State agreement, the Treaty, divided the Irish into two factions, 'pro-Treaty' and 'anti-Treaty', groups probably most closely identified today with the conservatively tinged Fine Gael party and the slightly more to centre Fianna Fáil. Unrest continued in the six northern counties, making difficult reunification of the island.

William Cosgrave, the leader of the Cumann na nGaedhal party (later Fine Gael) was in September 1922 elected President of the parliament of the new Free State. After his government had succeeded in ending the civil war, it had to face all the problems of peace. The army had to be demobilized, work found for the soldiers, and the institutions and buildings destroyed in the fighting

---

1. By Catherine MacCall and Börje Thilman.

had to be rebuilt. The large power plant at Ardnacrusha on the Shannon, constructed by Germans, became a symbol for the will to develop the country. New schools were built. Irish, the declining ancient tongue of the people, was decreed the national language in all schools, but its revival in fact proved difficult. At the same time a Puritan attitude coloured by nationalism and Catholicism impoverished the cultural climate. Many authors, among them the playwright Sean O'Casey left the country, and many who remained, looked elsewhere for publication.

The question of accepting the peace treaty and the terms of the Treaty with Great Britain dictated the trend of Irish politics for many years. The aim of the treaty, as far as the Irish were concerned, had been that the Catholic areas of the six counties near the boundary should be united with the Free State in accordance with the wishes of the inhabitants. This, however, did not materialise and the division along the old county boundaries, 'the Border' became a fact. Cosgrave, who as President signed the unsatisfactory Border agreement, was severely criticised for so doing.

The republicans of de Valera's party remained the political minority all during the 1920's. De Valera supporters in 1926 formed the Fianna Fáil (*i.e.* soldiers of destiny) party, but until 1927 these opponents of the Treaty did not take their seats in the parliament, Dáil Eireann. By joining the parliament formally, they expressed approval of the allegiance demanded in the 1922 Free State treaty, and so ended the parliamentary crisis that had continued since the Civil War.

At the end of the 1920's Ireland, in common with many other countries, suffered economic depression. Exports of foodstuffs to England diminished drastically and many factories closed down. There were signs of unrest in the country and thousands of IRA (Irish

Republican Army) men were jailed. De Valera's new party was at this stage linked to the revolutionaries, and with the aid of the small farmers, Fianna Fáil became the biggest party in the elections of 1932, gaining a majority of seats. De Valera was elected leader of the parliament and his party formed a new government.

During the 1930's de Valera in his turn had to declare the IRA an unlawful organisation and also declared illegal the Fascist movement known as the 'Blueshirts'. The so-called Economic war between Great Britain and Ireland, which took the form of exceptionally high tariff duties between the countries, was due to de Valera's decision to withold land annuity payments from Britain for the acquisition of landlords' titles. Only in 1938 this 'war' ended, and as part of the settlement England gave up its right to keep naval ships in the ports of Ireland.

De Valera and his energetic Minister of Industry Sean Lemass (later Taoiseach, or Prime Minister from 1959-66) worked to build up Irish industry. Agriculture was assisted and developed and reafforestation begun. State companies, such as The Irish Sugar Company, the Irish air line Aer Lingus, the turf or peat administration board, (Bord na Mona) and Irish Shipping were all formed during this period of economic expansion.

In 1937 a new Constitution was adopted in which Ireland was defined as a 'sovereign, independent, democratic state'. The concept of the Free State of Ireland was abandoned, and Ireland no longer sent delegates to the commonwealth conferences. Douglas Hyde, a leading Protestant figure in the Irish revival movement, was elected first president. The prime minister was given the Gaelic title of Taoiseach.

During the second world war Ireland took a neutral stand. The army of the country was equipped with Swedish and American weapons, and despite British and

American pressure de Valera declined to join the allied camp or to cede naval bases in Ireland. During the war years Ireland suffered severe shortages of certain food-stuffs and of raw materials for industry, and emigration to Great Britain increased greatly. Germany bombed Northern Ireland and Belfast was damaged.

In his victory speech Winston Churchill strongly criticised Ireland for having stayed out of the world war. Eamonn de Valera in his famous radio speech, answered:

'Mr. Churchill is proud of Britain's stand alone, after France had fallen and before America entered the war. Could he not find in his heart the generosity to acknow-ledge that there is a small nation that stood alone not for one year or two, but for several hundred years against aggression; that endured spoliations, famines, massacres in endless succession; that was clubbed many times into insensibility, but that each time on returning to con-sciousness took up the fight anew; a small nation that could never be got to accept defeat and has never surrendered her soul?'

In 1949 a coalition government which was headed by John A. Costello of Fine Gael declared that 'the state shall be called the Republic of Ireland'. The British govern-ment responded by declaring that Ireland had thereby excluded herself from membership of the Common-wealth. The declaration of the Republic did not greatly change the life of the Irish. They could still live and work in Britain as could the British in Ireland.

Although under pressure in 1949 to join the NATO agreement, the government of Ireland was not prepared to do so and declared that while it was in general agree-ment with the aims of NATO, it could not join this military alliance since British troops occupied six Irish counties. The crucial point there was that NATO guaranteed the integrity of the area of its member countries.

In 1955 Ireland joined the United Nations and Irish soldiers subsequently served with the UN peace-keeping forces in the Congo, Cyprus, the Sinai Desert and the Lebanon.

In 1959 Eamon de Valera retired as Prime Minister and was elected President of the Republic. When he died in 1975 at the age of 93 he had a record of almost 60 years as a central figure in the government and political life of Ireland. He was the son of a Spanish-American father and an Irish mother and was spared from the British execution squads in 1916 in spite of his role as a local commander in the Easter rebellion in Dublin. While he became the nation's most distinguished statesman, he retained many of the traits of a relentless revolutionary soldier and has been described as the controversial giant of modern Ireland.

De Valera's successor as Taoiseach was his collaborator of many years, Sean Lemass, who implemented a successful plan for economic development. During the first five-year plan from 1958 to 1963, 27,000 new industrial jobs were created. The Industrial Development Authority, an agency designed to promote economic development, has succeeded in attracting hundreds of foreign companies to Ireland where they have set up industries. Outside interest in Ireland was further stimulated when she joined the European Economic Community in 1973 with 83% of the voting population expressing their approval (in a national referendum).

*　　*　　*

Finally it is worth noting that the political life of free Ireland has been marked by a remarkable degree of stability. Since the establishment of the Free State in 1922

Ireland has had only nine different government leaders. Since ratification of the 1937 Constitution, there have been six Presidents: Douglas Hyde (1938-1945), Seán T. Ó'Ceallaigh (1945-1959), Eamon de Valera (1959-1973), Erskine Childers (1973-1974), Cearbhall Ó Dálaigh (1974-1976) and Patrick Hillery.

When Seamus MacCall died in 1964 A Little History of Ireland *was among his unpublished works in the form of an unrevised typescript and I undertook the revision and editing of his text for the first edition, issued in 1973.*

The reader will appreciate that Seamus MacCall's original text ended at the period of the Second Dáil and the book gives his personal view of the course of Ireland's history up to that time, written to present this view in a concise form.

The present edition contains a final chapter which I have added with the aid of a text prepared by Börje Thilman for his Finnish translation of the book, and I am deeply indebted to him for his interest and assistance.

I hope I have carried out Seamus MacCall's intention in preparing this text.

Catherine MacCall
1973, 1982.

INDEX

Act of Union, 36.
Apprentice Boys, 29.
Ard-Rí, 12.
Arms Act, 37.

Black and Tans, 45.
'Blueshirts', 53.

Catholic Emancipation, 37.
Catholic Relief Bills, 35, 37.
Celts, 7-9.
Charles I, 25, 26.
Charles II, 28.
Childers, Erskine, 51, 56.
Churchill, Winston, 47, 48, 54.
Citizen Army, 43.
Civil War, 50-52.
Coercion Acts, 37, 38.
Collins, Michael, 47, 51.
Colm Cille, 12.
Confederation of Kilkenny, 26.
Constitution (1937), 53.
Cosgrave, William T., 50, 51.
Costello, John A., 54.
Cumann na nGaedhal (Fine Gael), 51.

Dissenters, 34, 36.

Easter Rising (1916), 43, 44, 55.
Economic War, 53.
Edward VI, 20.
Elizabeth I, Queen, 21-23.
Emmet, Robert, 36.
Encumbered Estates Act, 41.
European Economic Community, 55.

Fenians, 39.
Fianna Fáil, 51-53.
Fine Gael, 51, 54.

Gauls, 7-9.
George II, 31.
Government, Republican, 44, 46.
Griffith, Arthur, 50.

Habeas Corpus Act, Suspension of, 37, 38.
Henry VII, 18.
Hillery, Patrick, 56.
Home Rule Bill, 41, 42.
Hyde, Douglas, 53, 56.

Industrial Development Authority, 55.
Iona, 12.
Irish Confederation, 38.
Irish Free State, 50-53.
Irish Republican Army (IRA), 44, 47, 52.
Irish Republican Brotherhood, 39, 43.
Irish Volunteers, 42, 43.

James I, 23.
James II, 28.

Larkin, James, 42.
Lemass, Seán, 53.
Limerick, Treaty of, 31.

Markiewicz, Countess de, 44.
Mary, Queen, 20, 21.
Mitchel, John, 38, 39.

N.A.T.O., 54.
Neutrality, 53, 54.
Normans, 16-17.
Norsemen, 14-16.

O'Ceallaigh, Sean T., 56.
O'Dalaigh, Cearbhall, 56.

Parliament, Irish, 33-34.
Partition, 46.
Patrick, St., 11.
Peace Conference, 48, 49.
Pearse, Patrick, 10, 43.

Peep o' Day Boys, 35.
Provisional Government, 50.
Republic, 54.
Romans, 11-12.

Sarsfield, Patrick, 30, 31.
Scotland, 10-12.

Taoiseach (Prime Minister), 53.
Tories, 21.
Treaty, 49-52.

United Irishmen, 35-36.
United Nations, 55.
Unlawful Oaths Act, 37.

Volunteers, 43-44.
de Valera, Eamon, 44, 48-56.

William of Orange, 28-31.

Young Irelanders, 38.

SEAMUS MAC CALL was born in 1892 and educated in Ireland, England and South America. He served with the British forces in the first World War but, because of his involvement in the Irish independence movement, resigned his British commission. He became an authority on Celtology and besides many articles in journals, published his major book, *And So Began the Irish Nation,* a study of the origin and evolution of the Celtic peoples in 1931. Among his other books were his novel, *Gods in Motley,* a biography of Thomas Moore and *Irish Mitchell,* which appeared in 1937. He served in the Irish army from 1940 to 1946. Seamus MacCall devoted his later years to book reviewing and other occasional writings. In 1963 he was elected Chairman of Irish PEN. He died in 1964.